Anonymous

War Songs, for Anniversaries and Gatherings of Soldiers

To Which is Added a Selection of Songs and Hymns for Memorial Day

Anonymous

War Songs, for Anniversaries and Gatherings of Soldiers
To Which is Added a Selection of Songs and Hymns for Memorial Day

ISBN/EAN: 9783337135935

Printed in Europe, USA, Canada, Australia, Japan

Cover: Foto ©Thomas Meinert / pixelio.de

More available books at **www.hansebooks.com**

Dedicated to the

G. A. R.

———

WAR SONGS,

FOR

Anniversaries and Gatherings of Soldiers,

TO WHICH IS ADDED A SELECTION OF

SONGS AND HYMNS

FOR

MEMORIAL DAY.

THE CHORUSES OF ALL THE SONGS ARE ARRANGED FOR

MALE VOICES.

———

BOSTON:
Copyright, 1883 by
OLIVER DITSON & CO.

C. H. DITSON & CO.,   LYON & HEALY,   J. E. DITSON & CO.,
NEW YORK.   CHICAGO.   PHILADELPHIA.

CONTENTS.

J. FRANK GILES, MUSIC STEREOTYPER AND PRINTER, BOSTON.

WAR SONGS.

TENTING ON THE OLD CAMP GROUND.

Words and Music by WALTER KITTREDGE.   Arranged by M. F. H. SMITH.

Tempo di Marcia.
REVEILLE.

1. We're tent-ing to-night on the old Camp ground.
2. We've been tenting to-night on the old Camp ground.
3. We are tired of war on the old Camp ground.
4. We've been fighting to day on the old Camp ground.

Give us a song to cheer   Our wea-ry hearts, a song of home, And friends we love so dear
Thinking of days gone by, Of the lov'd ones at home that gave us the hand, And the tear that said "good-bye!"
Ma-ny are dead and gone, Of the brave and true who've left their homes, Others been wounded long.
Ma-ny are ly-ing near: Some are dead, and some are dying, Many are in tears.

CHORUS.

Many are the hearts that are weary to-night, Wishing for the war to cease, Many are the hearts, looking for the right, To

last time pp.

see the dawn of peace. Tenting to-night, tenting to-night, Tenting on the old camp ground, Dying on the old camp ground.

last verse. Dying to-night. dying to-night,

DO THEY MISS ME AT HOME?

Music by S. M. GRANNIS.

1. Do they miss me at home, do they
2. When twi - light approaches, the

miss me? 'Twould be an as - surance most dear, To know that this moment some
sea - son That ev - er is sa - cred to song, Does some one re - peat my name

loved one, Were say - ing, I wish he were here; To feel that the group at the
o - ver, And sigh that I tar - ry so long? And is there a chord in the

fire - side, Were thinking of me as I roam, Oh yes, 'twould be joy beyond
mu - sic, That's miss'd when my voice is a- way, And a chord in each heart that a -

ad lib.

measure To know that they miss'd me at home, To know that they miss'd me at
waketh Re - gret at my wea - ri - some stay, Re - gret at my wea - ri - some

home.
stay.

3 Do they set me a chair near the table
　When ev'ning's home pleasures are nigh,
When the candles are lit in the parlor,
　And the stars in the calm azure sky?
And when the " good nights" are repeated,
　And all lay them down to their sleep,
Do they think of the absent, and waft me
　A whispered " good night" while they weep?

4 Do they miss me at home—do they miss me
　At morning, at noon, or at night?
And lingers one gloomy shade round them
　That only my presence can light?
Are joys less invitingly welcome,
　And pleasures less hale than before,
Because one is missed from the circle,
　Because I am with them no more?

KINGDOM COMING.

Words and Music by HENRY C. WORK.

1. Say, darkeys, hab you seen de massa, Wid de muffstas on his face, Go
2. He six foot one way, two foot tudder, An' he weigh tree hundred pound, His

long de road some time dis mornin', Like he gwine to leab de place? He seen a smoke, way
coat so big he couldn't pay de tailor, An' it won't go half way round. He drill so much dey

up de ribber, Whar de Limkum gumboats lay; He took his hat, an' lef berry sudden, An' I
call him Cap'an, An' he get so drefful tann'd, I spec he try an' fool dem Yankees For to

CHORUS.

spec he's run a-way! De mas-sa run, ha! ha! De dar-keys stay, ho!
tink he's con-tra-band.

ho! It mus' be now de kingdom coming, An' de year ob Ju-bi-lo!

3 De darkeys feel so lonesome, libing
   In de log-house on de lawn,
Dey move dar tings to massa's parlor,
   For to keep it while he's gone.
Dar's wine an' cider in de kitchen,
   An' de darkeys dey'll hab some ;
I spose dey'll all be confiscated,
   When de Linkum sojers come.

4 De oberseer he make us trouble,
   An' he dribe us round a spell ;
We lock him up in de smoke-house cellar,
   Wid de key trown in de well.
De whip is lost, de han'-cuff broken,.
   But de massa'll hab his pay ;
He's ole enough, big enough, ought to known·
   Dan to went an' run away.   [better,

BABYLON IS FALLEN!

SEQUEL TO "KINGDOM COMING."

Words and Music by HENRY C. WORK. No. 21.

1. Don't you see de black clouds Ris-in' o - ber yonder, Whar de Massa's ole plantation am?
2. Don't you see de lightnin' Flashin' in de canebrake, Like as if we're gwine to hab a storm?
3. Way up in de cornfield, Whar you hear de tunder, Dat is our ole for-ty-pounder gun;

Neb-ber you be frightened, Dem is on-ly dar - keys, Come to jine an' fight for Uncle Sam.
No! you is mis-tak - en, 'Tis de darkey's bay'nets, An' de buttons on dar u - ni-form.
When de shells are miss-in', Den we load wid punkins, All de same to make de cowards run.

CHORUS.
1st. Tenor.

Look out dar, now! We's a gwine to shoot, Look out dar, don't you understand?

2d. Tenor.

Look out dar, now! We's a gwine to shoot, Look out dar, don't you understand?

1st. Bass.

Look out dar, now! We's a gwine to shoot, Look out dar, don't you understand?

2d. Bass.

O, don't you know dat

Repeat Chorus softly.

Bab-y-lon is fall-en! Bab-y-lon is fall-en! And we's a gwine to oc-cu-py de land.

Bab-y-lon is fall-en! Bab-y-lon is fall-en! And we's a gwine to oc-cu-py de land.

Bab-y-lon is fall-en! Bab-y-lon is fall-en! And we's a gwine to oc-cu-py de land.

4 Massa was de Kernel
In de rebel army,
Ebber sence he went an' run away;
But his lubly darkeys,
Dey has been a watchin',
An' dey take him pris'ner tudder day.
CHO.—Look out dar, &c.

5 We will be de massa,—
He will be de sarvant—
Try him how he like it for a spell;
So we crack de Butt'nuts.
So we take de Kernel,
So de cannon carry back de shell.
CHO.—Look out dar, &c

BRAVE BOYS ARE THEY!

DUET AND CHORUS.

Words and Music by HENRY C. WORK.

Not too fast.

Give the quarter notes their full time, with strongly marked accent.

1. Heav - i - ly falls the rain,...... Wild are the breez - es to - night ; But
2. Un - der the home-stead roof,...... Nest - led so co - zy and warm, While
3. Think-ing no less of them,...... Lov - ing our coun - try the more, We
4. May the bright wings of love,...... Guard them wher - ev - er they roam ; The

ritard.

'neath the roof, the hours as they fly, Are hap-py, and calm, and bright.....
sol - diers sleep, with lit - tle or naught, To shelter them from the storm......
sent them forth to fight for the flag, Their fa-thers be - fore them bore......
time has come when brothers must fight, And sis-ters must pray at home......

ritard.

Gath - er-ing round our fire - side, Tho' it be sum - mer time, We
Rest - ing on gras - sy couch - es, Pil-low'd on hil - locks damp ; Of
Tho' the great tear-drops start - ed, This was our part - ing trust ; "God
Oh! the dread field of bat - tle! Soon to be strewn with graves ! It

sit and talk of brothers a-broad, For-getting the mid-night chime......
mar-tial fare, how lit-tle we know, Till brothers are in the camp......
bless you boys! we'll wel-come you home, When rebels are in the dust."......
broth-ers fall, then bu-ry them where Our ban-ner in tri-umph waves......

CHORUS

Brave boys are they!.... Gone at their coun-try's call, And

Brave boys are they!.... Gone at their coun-try's call, And

yet, and yet we can-not for-get, That many brave boys must fall......

yet, and yet we can-not for-get, That many brave boys must fall......

SHERMAN'S MARCH TO THE SEA.

Written and Composed in Prison, at Columbia, South Carolina, and Dedicated to the Army of the Union.

Words by Lieut. S. H. M. BYERS.

Music by Lieut. J. O. ROCKWELL.

Arranged by A. E. WIMMERSTEDT.

1. Our camp-fire shone bright on the mountains That frown'd on the river be-low, While we stood by our guns in the morning and ea-ger-ly watch'd for the foe; When a rid-er came out from the darkness, That hur g o-ver mountain and tree,

And shouted, "boys, up and be rea-dy, For Sherman will march to the sea,"

And shouted, "boys, up and be rea-dy, For Sher-man will march to the sea."

2 Then cheer upon cheer, for bold Sherman
  Went up from each valley and glen,
And the bugles re-echoed the music
  That came from the lips of the men;
For we knew that the stars on our banner
  More bright in their splendor would be,
And that blessings from Northland would greet us
  When Sherman marched down to the sea.

3 Then forward, boys, forward to battle
  We marched on our wearisome way,
And we stormed the wild hills of Resacca
  God bless those who fell on that day:
Then Kennesaw, dark in its glory,
  Frowned down on the flag of the free;
But the East and the West bore our standards,
  And Sherman marched on to the sea.

4 Still onward we pressed, till our banner
  Swept out from Atlanta's grim walls,
And the blood of the patriot dampened
  The soil where the traitor flag falls;
But we paused not to weep for the fallen,
  Who slept by each river and tree,
Yet we twined them a wreath of the laurel
  As Sherman marched down to the sea.

5 Oh, proud was our army that morning,
  That stood where the pine proudly towers,
When Sherman said, "boys, you are weary;
  This day fair Savaurah is ours!"
Then sang we a song for our chieftain,
  That echoed o'er river and lea,
And the stars in our banner shone brighter,
  When Sherman marched down to the sea.

GLORY! GLORY! HALLELUJAH!

1. John Brown's bo-dy lies a
2. The stars of Heaven are

mould'ring in the grave, John Brown's bo-dy lies a mould'ring in the grave,
look-ing kind-ly down, The stars of Heaven are look-ing kind-ly down, The

John Brown's bo-dy lies a mould'ring in the grave, His soul is marching on.
stars of Heaven are look-ing kind-ly down, On the grave of old John Brown.

3 ‖: He's gone to be a soldier in the army of the Lord! :‖
His soul is marching on.

4 ‖: John Brown's knapsack is strapped upon his back. :‖
His soul is marching on.

5 ‖: His pet lambs will meet him on the way, :‖
And they'll go marching on.

6 ‖: They will hang Jeff Davis to a tree ‖
As they march along.

CHORUS.

Glo - ry! glo - ry hal - le - lu - jah!   Glo - ry! glo - ry hal - le - lu - jah!

Glo - ry! glo - ry hal - le - lu - jah!   Glo - ry! glo - ry hal - le - lu - jah!

Glo - ry! glo - ry hal - le - lu - jah!   His soul is march-ing on.

Glo - ry! glo - ry hal - le - lu - jah!   His soul is marching on.

BATTLE HYMN OF THE REPUBLIC.

1 Mine eyes have seen the glory of the coming of the
       Lord ;
   He is trampling out the vintage where the grapes of
       wrath are stored ;
   He hath loosed the fateful lightning of His terrible
       swift sword ;
           His truth is marching on.

2 I have seen Him in the watch-fires of a hundred
       circling camps,
   They have builded Him an altar in the evening dews
       and damps ;
   I can read His righteous sentence by the dim and
       flaring lamps ;
           His day is marching on.

3 I have read a fiery gospel writ in burnished rows of
       steel ;
   "As ye deal with my contemners, so with you my
       grace shall deal ;"

Let the Hero, born of woman crush the serpent
       with his heel,
           Since God is marching on.

4 He has sounded forth the trumpet that shall never
       call retreat ;
   He is sifting out the hearts of men before His judg-
       ment seat ;
   Oh, he swift, my soul, to answer Him ! be jubilant,
       my feet !
           Our God is marching on.

5 In the beauty of the lillies Christ was born across
       the sea,
   With a glory in his bosom that transfigures you and
       me ;
   As he died to make men holy, let us die to make
       men free,
           While God is marching on.

WE OLD BOYS.

Words and Music by JOHN L. PARKER.

Marching time.

1. 'Twas side by side as comrades dear, In
2. And tho' thro' all these years of peace, We've
3. What if grim age creeps on a-pace, Our

dark days long a - go,   We fought the fight with-out a fear, And rendered blow for
somewhat old - er grown, The spir - it of those ear- ly days, We'll ev - er proud-ly
souls shall not grow old, But we will stand as in the days When we were warriors

blow.   In bat - tle, march, or pris - on   pen, Each un - to each was
own.   Our grand old flag is just as fair, As in the try - ing
bold.   We stood for right—for our dear land, For home, and all that's

true,   As beard-less boys became strong men, And brav'd the long war through.
time,   When trai-tors sought its folds to tear, And we suppressed the crime.
true,   So firm-ly clasp hand un-to hand, And com-radeship re-new.

CHORUS.

1st & 2d Tenor.

We are the boys, the gay old boys, Who marched in Six-ty-

1st & 2d Bass.

- one; We'll ne'er for-get old times, my boys, When you and I were young.

ORIGIN OF YANKEE DOODLE.—In the summer of 1775, the British army, under command of Abercrombie, lay encamped on the east bank of the Hudson river, a little south of the city of Albany, awaiting reinforcements of militia from the Eastern States, previous to marching on Ticonderoga. During the month of June these raw levies poured into camp, company after company, each man differently armed, equipped and accoutred from his neighbor, and the whole presenting such a spectacle as was never equalled, unless by the celebrated regiment of merry Jack Falstaff. Their *outré* appearance furnished great amusement to the British officers. One Dr. Shamburg, an English surgeon, composed the tune of Yankee Doodle, and arranged it to words, which were gravely dedicated to the new recruits. The joke took, and the tune has come down to this day. The original words, which we take from Farmer and Moore's "Historical Collections," published in 1820, we have not, however, met with before in many years.

1. Fa-ther and I went down to camp, A-long with Captain Good-win, And there we saw the
2. And there was Captain Washington Up-on a slapping stal - lion, And giv - ing or-ders
3. And then the feathers on his hat, They looked so tarnal fine - y, I want-ed pes-ki-
4. And there they had a swamping gun, As big as a log of ma-ple, On a deu-ced

men and boys, As thick as has-ty pud-ding. Yan-kee Doo-dle Keep it up,
to his men, I guess there was a mil-lion. Yan-kee Doo-dle Keep it up,
-ly to get, To give to my Je-mi-ma. Yan-kee Doo-dle Keep it up,
lit-tle cart, A load for fa-ther's cat-tle. Yan-kee Doo-dle Keep it up,

Yan-kee Doodle dan-dy. Mind the Music and the step, And with the girls be handy.

5 And every time they fired it off
  It took a horn of powder;
  It made a noise like father's gun,
  Only a nation louder.

6 I went as near to it myself,
  As Jacob's underpinin',
  And father went as near again—
  I thought the deuce was in him.

7 (It scared me so I ran the streets,
  Nor stopped as I remember,
  Till I got home, and safely locked
  In granny's little chamber.)

8 And there I see a little keg,
  Its heads were made of leather,
  They knocked upon't with little sticks,
  To call the folks together.

9 And there they'd fife away like fun,
  And play on corn stalk fiddles,
  And some had ribbons red as blood,
  All bound around their middles.

10 The troopers too, would gallop up,
   And fire right in our faces;
   It scared me almost half to death
   To see them run such races.

11 Uncle Sam came there to change
   Some pancakes and some onions,
   For 'lasses cakes to carry home
   To give his wife and young ones.

12 But I can't tell you half I see,
   They kept up such a smother;
   So I took my hat off, made a bow,
   And scampered home to mother.

OLE SHADY.

THE SONG OF THE CONTRABAND.

Music by B. R. HANBY.

1. Oh! yah! yah! darkies laugh wid me, For de white folks say Ole Sha - dy's free; So don't you see dat de ju - bi - lee Is a - coming, coming, Hail! migh- ty day.

Den a - way, away, for I can't wait a - ny longer, Hoo - ray, hooray, I'm going home.

Den a - way, away, for I can't wait a - ny longer, Hoo - ray, hooray, I'm going home.

2 Oh, Mass' got scared and so did his lady,
Dis chile breaks for Ole Uncle Aby,
" Open de gates out, here's Ole Shady
A coming, coming,"
Hail! mighty day.

3 Good bye Mass' Jeff, good bye Mis'r Stephens,
'Scuse dis niggah for takin his leavins,
'Spect pretty soor you'l hear
Uncle Abram's coming, coming,
Hail! mighty day.

4 Good bye, hard work wid never any pay,
Ise a gwine up North where the good folks say
Dat white wheat bread and a dollara day,
Are coming, coming,
Hail! mighty day.

5 Oh, I've got a wife, and I've got a baby,
Living up yonder in Lower *Canady*,
Wont dey laugh when dey see Ole Shady
A coming, coming,
Hail! mighty day

OLD FOLKS AT HOME.

As sung by E. P. CHRISTY.   Written and Comp sed by S. C. FOSTER.

Moderato.

1. Way down up on de Swa - nee rib - ber, Far, far a -
2. All round de lit- tle farm I wander'd When I was
3. One lit - tle hut a - mong de bush- es, One dat I

way,   Dere's wha' my heart is turn - ing eb - er, Dere's wha' de old folks stay.
young, Den man- y hap- py days I squander'd, man - y de songs I sung.
love, Still sad- ly to my mem.'ry rush- es, No mat- ter where I rove.

All   up and down de whole cre - a - tion Sad - ly I roam,
When I was play- ing wid my brud- der, Hap - py was I
When will I see de bees a hum- ming, All round de comb?

Still   longing for de old plan-ta-tion, And for de old folks at home.
Oh!   take me to my kind old mud-der, Dere let me live and   die.
When   will I hear de ban-jo tumming, Down in my good old   home.

CHORUS.
1st & 2d TENORS.

All   de world am   sad and drea-ry, Eb-ry-where I   roam.
1st & 2d BASSES.

Oh! darkies, how my heart grows wea-ry, Far from de old folks at home.
Melody.

MASSA'S IN DE COLD COLD GROUND.

Words and Music by STEPHEN C FOSTER.

poco lento.

1. Round de meadows am a ring - ing   De Darkey's mournful song,   'Twas
2. When   de autumn leaves were fall - ing,   When de days were cold,   'Twas
3. Mas - sa make de dar-keys love him,   Cayse he was so kind,

While   de mocking bird am sing - ing,   Hap - py as de day   am   long.
hard   to   hear old mas-sa call - ing,   Cayse he was so weak and   old.
Now,   dey sad-ly weep a-bove   him,   Mourning cayse he leave dem behind.   I

Where de i - vy am   a creep - ing,   O'er de gras - sy mound,
Now   de orange tree am bloom- ing,   On de sand - y shore,
can - not work be - fore to - mor - row,   Cayse de tear - drop flow,   I

Dare old mas-sa am a sleep - ing, Sleep-ing in de cold, cold ground.
Now de summer days am com - ing, Mas - sa nebber calls no more.
try to drive a - way my sor - row, Pick - in' on de old ban - jo.

CHORUS.

Down in de corn - field, Hear dat mourn-ful sound!

All de darkeys am a weep-ing, Mas-sa's in de cold, cold ground.

WHEN JOHNNY COMES MARCHING HOME.

Words and Music by LOUIS LAMBERT.

With spirit.

SOLO.

CHORUS.

1. When Johnny comes march-ing home   a - gain,   Hur - rah,..... ...   hur
2. The old   church bell   will   peal   with   joy,   Hur - rah,........   hur-
3. Get   rea - dy   for   the   Ju - bi - lee,   Hur - rah,........   hur-
4. Let   love   and   friend - ship   on   that   day,   Hur - rah,..... ..   hur-

Solo.   **Chorus.**   **Solo.**

- rah ! We'll give him a heart - y wel -come then, Hur - rah, hur - rah ! The
- rah ! To wel - come home our dar - ling boy, Hur - rah, hur - rah ! The
- rah ! We'll give the he - ro three times three, Hur - rah, hur - rah ! The
- rah ! Their choic - est treas -ures then dis - play, Hur - rah, hur - rah ! And

men will cheer, the boys will shout, the la - dies, they will all turn out,
vil - lage lads and las - sies say, With ro - ses they will strew the way,
lau - rel wreath is rea - dy now To place up - on his loy - al brow,
let each one per - form some part, To fill with joy the war -rior's heart,

Chorus

And we'll all feel gay when John - ny comes march - ing home.

COLUMBIA, THE GEM OF THE OCEAN,

OR THE RED, WHITE AND BLUE.

Maestoso.

Words and Music by DAVID T SHAW.

1. O Co-lum-bia! the gem of the o-cean, The home of the brave and the free, The
2. When war winged it wide des-o-la-tion, And threatened the land to de-form, The
3. The wine-cup, the wine-cup bring hither, And fill you it true to the brim, May

shrine of each pa-triot's de votion, A world of-fers homage to thee. Thy
ark then of freedom's foundation, Co-lum-bia, rode safe thro' the storm ; With
the wreaths they have won never wither, Nor the star of their glory grow dim ! May

man-dates make he-roes assemble, When Lib er-ty's form stands in view, Thy
her garlands of vict'ry around her, When so proudly she bore her brave crew, With
the ser-vice u-nited ne'er sever, But they to their col-ors prove true ! The

banners make ty - ran- ny tremble, When borne by the red, white and blue.
her flag proud-ly floating before her, The boast of the red, white and blue.
Ar-my and Na - vy for - ev- er, Three cheers for the red, white and blue.

CHORUS.

When borne by the red,white and blue, When borne by the red,white and blue, Thy

banners make ty - ra - ny tremble, When borne by the red, white and blue.

MARCHING THROUGH GEORGIA.

Words and Music by HENRY C. WORK.

INTRODUCTION.

1. Bring the good old bugle, boys! we'll sing an-oth-er song— Sing it with a spir-it that will
2. How the darkies shouted when they heard the joy-ful sound! How the turkeys gobbled which our
3. Yes, and there were Un-ion men who wept with joy-ful tears, When they saw the hon-or'd flag they
4. "Sherman's dashing Yankee boys will nev-er reach the coast!" So the sau-cy reb-els said, and
5. So we made a thoroughfare for Freedom and her train, Six-ty miles in la-titude—three

start the world a-long— Sing it as we used to sing it, fif-ty thous-and strong,
com-mis-sa-ry found! How the sweet po-ta-toes e-ven start-ed from the ground,
had not seen for years; Hard-ly could they be restrained from breaking forth in cheers,
'twas a hand-some boast, Had they not for-got a-las! to reck-on with the host,
hun-dred to the main; Trea-son fled be-fore us, for re-sistance was in vain,

While we were march-ing through Geor - gia. Hur - rah! hur - rah! We bring the ju - bi - lee! Hur - rah! hur - rah! the flag that makes you free! So we sang the cho-rus from At - lan- ta to the sea, While we were marching thro' Geor - gia.

POOR OLD SLAVE.

Arranged by E. M. F.

By E. W. FOSTER.

Legato.

1. 'Tis just one year a-go to-day, That I re-mem-ber well, I sat down by poor Nel-ly's side And a sto-ry she did tell. 'Twas 'bout a poor un-hap-py slave, That lived for ma-ny a year; But
2. She took my arm, we walk'd a-long In-to an o-pen field, And there she paused to breathe a-while, Then to his grave did steal. She sat down by that lit-tle mound, And soft-ly whispered there, Come
3. But since that time how things have chang'd! Poor Nelly that was my bride, Is laid be-neath the cold grave sod, With her fa-ther by her side. I plant-ed there up-on her grave, The weep-ing wil-low tree; I

now he's dead, and in his grave, No mas - ter does he fear.
to me, fa - ther, 'tis thy child, Then gent - ly dropp'd a tear.
bathed its roots with ma - ny a tear, That it might shel - ter me.

CHORUS.

Legato.

The poor old slave has gone to rest, We know that he is free;

Dis - turb him not but let him rest, Way down in Ten - ne - see.

THE BATTLE CRY OF FREEDOM.

RALLYING SONG.

Words and Music by GEO. F. ROOT

1. Yes, we'll
2. We are
3. We will
4. So we're

CHORUS.

ral - ly round the flag, boys, we'll ral-ly once again, Shouting the bat-tle-cry of Freedom, We will
springing to the call of our Brothers gone before, Shouting the bat-tle-cry of Freedom, And we'll
welcome to our num-bers the loy-al true and brave, Shouting the bat-tle-cry of Freedom, And al-
springing to the call from the East and from the West, Shouting the bat-tle-cry of Freedom, And we'll

CHORUS.

ral - ly from the hill-side, we'll gath - er from the plain, Shouting the bat-tle cry of Free - dom.
fill the va-cant ranks with a mil - lion freemen more, Shouting the bat-tle cry of Free - dom.
tho' they may be poor not a man shall be a slave, Shouting the bat-tle cry of Free - dom
hurl the reb - el crew from the land we love the best, Shouting the bat-tle cry of Free - dom.

CHORUS.
Fortissimo.

The Un-ion for-ev-er, Hur-rah boys, hurrah! Down with the traitor, Up with the star, While we

The Un-ion for-ev-er, Hur-rah boys, hurrah! Down with the traitor, Up with the star, While we

ral-ly round the flag, boys, ral-ly once again, Shouting the bat-tle cry of Free-dom.

ral-ly round the flag, boys, ral-ly once again, Shouting the bat-tle cry of Free-dom.

THE BATTLE-CRY OF FREEDOM.

(BATTLE SONG.)

1 We are marching to the field, boys, we're going to the fight,
Shouting the battle-cry of Freedom,
And we bear the glorious stars for the Union and the right,
Shouting the battle-cry of Freedom.

Cho.—The Union forever, hurrah! boys, hurrah!
Down with the traitor, up the star,
For we're marching to the field boys, going to the fight,
Shouting the battle-cry of Freedom!

2 We will meet the rebel host, boys, with fearless heart and true,
Shouting the battle-cry of Freedom,

And we'll show what Uncle Sam has for loyal men to do,
Shouting the battle-cry of Freedom.

3 If we fall amid the fray, boys, we'll face them to the last,
Shouting the battle-cry of Freedom,
And our comrades brave shall hear us, as they go rushing past,
Shouting the battle-cry of Freedom.

4 Yes, for L'berty and Union we're springing to the fight,
Shouting the battle-cry of Freedom,
And the vict'ry shall be ours, for we're rising in our might,
Shouting the battle-cry of Freedom.

THE STAR SPANGLED BANNER.

With an additional verse (5th), by DR. O. W. HOLMES.

Con spirito.

5. When our land is il - lum'd with lib - er - ty's smile, If a foe from with -

1. Oh! say can you see, by the dawn's ear - ly light, What so proud - ly we
2. On the shore, dim - ly seen thro' the mist of the deep, Where the foe's haughty
3. And where is that band, who so vaunt - ing - ly swore, 'Mid the hav - oc of
4. Oh! thus be it ev - er when free - men shall stand, Be - tween their lov'd

in strike a blow at her glo -ry, Down, down with the traitor, that dares to de -

hail'd at the twilight's last gleaming, Whose stripes and bright stars, thro' the per - il - ous
host in dread si - lence re - pos-es, What is that which the breeze, o'er the tow - er - ing
war and the bat - tle's con - fusion, A home and a coun - try they'd leave us no
home and the war's des - o - lation, Blest with vic - t'ry and peace, may the heav'n rescued

- file The flag of her stars and the page of her sto - ry! By the mil - lions un-

fight, O'er the ram - parts we watch'd, were so gal - lant - ly streaming; And the rock - et's red
steep, As it fit - ful - ly blows, half con - ceals, half dis - clos - es? Now it catch - es the
more? Their blood has wash'd out their foul footstep's po - lu - tion; No re - fuge could
land, Praise the Pow'r that hath made and preserved us a na - tion. Then con - quer we

chain'd who our birth - right have gain'd, We will keep her bright bla - zon for - ev - er   unstain'd!

glare, the bombs bursting   in   air,   Gave   proof thro' the night that our   flag was   still there!
gleam   of   the morning's first beam, In full glo - ry re - flect - ed, now shines in   the stream:
save   the hire - ling and slave From the ter - ror of flight or the gloom of   the grave,
must, when our cause it   is   just, And   this   be our mot - to, "In God   is   our trust,"

CHORUS.

1. Oh !   say,   does   that   star   span - gled   ban -   ner   yet
2. 'Tis the   star   span - gled   ban - ner,   oh !   long   may   it

3. And the   star   span - gled   ban - ner   in   tri - umph   shall
4,5. And the   star   span - gled   ban - ner   in   tri - umph   shall

1,2,3. wave,   O'er the land   of   the   free   and   the home   of   the brave !

4,5. wave,   While the land   of   the   free,   is   the home   of   the brave !

TRAMP! TRAMP! TRAMP!

THE PRISONER'S HOPE.

Words and Music by GEO. F. ROOT.

Tempo di Marcia.

1. In the
2. In the
3. So with

prison cell I sit, Thinking mother, dear, of you, And our bright and happy home so far away, And the
battle front we stood When their fiercest charge they made, And they swept us off a hundred men or more, But be
-in the pris-on cell, We are waiting for the day That shall come to o-pen wide the iron door, And the

tears they fill my eyes Spite of all that I can do, Tho' I try to cheer my comrades and be gay.
-fore we reach'd their lines, They were beaten back dismay'd, And we heard the cry of vict'ry o'er and o'er.
hollow eye grows bright, And the poor heart almost gay, As we think of seeing home and friends once more.

When the Chorus is sung, this may be omitted after the first verse.

Tramp, tramp, tramp, the boys are march - ing, Cheer up comrades they will come, And be

When the chorus is not sung, end here.

- neath the star-ry flag We will breathe the air a-gain Of the freeland in our own be-lov-ed home.

CHORUS.

Tramp, tramp, tramp, the boys are march - ing,   Cheer up, comrades, they will come,   And be -

Cheer up, com - rades,   they will come,

Tramp, tramp, tramp, the boys are marching on, O, cheer up, com - rades,   they will come, And be -

- neath the star- ry flag We shall breathe the air a-gain Of the freeland in our own belov - ed home.

- neath the star- ry flag We shall breathe the air a-gain Of the freeland in our own belov- ed home.

THE ARTILLERIST'S OATH.

C. F. ADAMS.

Alla Marcia.

1. From out the wild flame of the fur-nace, Thou cams't with la-bor fierce and earnest; As the
2. Thou art my bride, my stern faith swearing, True love to thee my heart is bear-ing; As the

glo - ry of a queen, O can - non, is thy sheen; On thee in oath I
song of night-in - gale, Borne on zeph - yrs o'er the vale, Thy voice can make my

dim.

lay my hand, True hold I out, true hold I out, With thee to fight, With thee to
heart to bound. With thee my song, with thee my song, In ev-'ry hour, In ev-'ry

True hold I out, With thee to
With thee my song, In ev-'ry

True hold I out, With thee to
With thee my song, In ev - 'ry

fight, For home, for freedom, Fa - ther-land, For
fight, In ech - o loud-ly shall resound, In

fight, For home, for freedom, Fa - therland,
fight, In ech - o loud-ly shall resound,

home, for free-dom, Fa - ther-land, For Fa - - - - ther- land.
ech - o loud-ly shall re-sound, In ech - - - - o sound.

For home, for free-dom, Fa - ther-land.
In ech - o loud - ly shall resound.

3 Soon for the wedding feast adorning,
A veil of silver grey, like morning,
Shall, wreathed with laurels, shine
Upon thy brow sublime.
And thee, amid the echoing horn,
The bullet song, the bullet song,
The sabre clash, the sabre clash,
I'll wed thee in the battle's storm.

4 And when is come the hour of dying,
The fire of life's weak match is flying,
I'd crawl to thy rent side
And there, with heartfelt pride,
Shout, while the breech supports my hand—
True held I out, true held I out,
With thee to fight, with thee to fight,
For home, for freedom, Fatherland.

SONG.

Music by H. COYLE.

1. All qui - et a - long the Po - to - mac, they say, Ex - cept now and then a stray Pick - et Is
2. All qui - et a - long the Po - to - mac to- - night, Where the sol - diers lie peace - ful - ly dreaming, Their
3. There's on - ly the sound of the lone sentry's tread, As he tramps from the rock to the fountain, And

shot on his beat as he walks to and fro, By a ri - fle - man
tents in the rays of the clear autumn moon, Or the light of the
thinks of the two in the low trun-dle bed, Far a - way in the

*

hid in a thicket. 'Tis nothing, a pri - vate or two now and
watch-fires are gleaming. A trem - u - lous sigh, as the gen - tle night-
cot on the mountain. His musket falls slack, and his face dark and

then, Will not count in the news of the bat-tle: Not an
- wind, Through the for - est leaves soft - ly is creeping ; While
grim, Grows gen - tle with mem - o - ries ten-der, As he

Of - fi - cer lost, on - ly one of the men Moaning out all a-
-stars up a - bove, with their glit - ter - ing eyes, Keep guard, for the
mut - ters a prayer for the chil - dren a - sleep, For their mother, may

- lone the death - rat - tle. ....
ar - my is sleep - ing. ....
heav - en de - fend her. ....

For last four lines go to *.

4 The moon seems to shine just as brightly as then,
   That night when the love yet unspoken
Leaped up to his lips—when low murmured vows
   Were pledged to be ever unbroken.
Then drawing his sleeve roughly over his eyes,
   He dashes off tears that are welling,
And gathers his gun closer to its place,
   As if to keep down the heart-swelling.

5 He passes the fountain, the blasted pine tree,
   The footstep is lagging and weary;
Yet onward he goes through the broad belt of light,
   Toward the shades of the forest so dreary.
Hark! was it the night-wind that rustled the leaves?
   Was it moon-light so wondrously flashing?
It looked like a rifle—HA! MARY, good-bye!
   And the life-blood is ebbing and plashing.

6 All quiet along the Potomac to-night,
   No sound save the rush of the river;
While soft falls the dew on the face of the dead,
   The picket's off duty forever!

JUST BEFORE THE BATTLE, MOTHER.

Words and Music by GEO. F. ROOT.

1. Just be-fore the bat-tle, Moth-er,   I am thinking most of you,
2. Oh, I long to see you, Moth-er,   And the lov- ing ones at home,
3. Hark! I hear the bu- gles sounding,   'Tis the sig - nal for the fight,

While up- on the field we're watching,   With the en - e - my in view—
But I'll never leave our ban- ner,   Till in hon - or I   can come,
Now, may God protect us, Moth-er,   As   he ev - er does the right.

Comrades brave are round me lying,   Fill'd with thot's of home and God;   For
Tell the traitors, all around you,   That their cru-el words we know,   In
Hear the "Bat-tle-Cry of Freedom,"*   How it swells up- on the air,   Oh,

well they know that on the mor-row,   Some will sleep be-neath the sod.
ev' - ry bat - tle kill our sol-diers,   By the help they give the foe.
yes, we'll ral - ly round the standard,   Or we'll per - ish no- bly there.

* In some of the divisions of our army the "Battle-Cry" is sung, when going into action, by order of commanding officers.

CHORUS.

Fare - well, Moth - er, you may nev - er,

TENORS.

Fare - well, Moth - er, you may nev - er, you may nev - er, Moth - er,

BASSES.

But Oh, you'll not for - get me,

press me to your heart a - gain,........ But, Oh, you'll not for - get me,

Moth - er,

Repeat, pp.

Moth - er, you will not for - get me, If I'm num - ber'd with the slain.

RALLY ROUND THE FLAG.

Music by WM. B. BRADBURY.

Allegro con spirito.

1. Ral -ly round the flag, boys, Give it to the breeze, That's the banner we love,
2. Their flag is but a rag, Ours is the true one, Up with the stars and stripes,

On the land and seas; Brave hearts are un- der ours, Let the traitor brag,
Down with the new one! Brave hearts are un- der ours, &c.

Gallant lads, fire away! And fight for the flag! Gallant lads, fire away! And fight for the flag!

Ral - ly round the flag, boys,   Give it to   the breeze,   That's the banner we love,

On the land and seas;   Let our colors fly, boys, Guard them day and night, For

Vic -to-ry is lib - er-ty, And God will bless the right! Then ral- ly round the flag, boys,

Ral - ly round, ral - ly round, Ral - ly round the flag, boys, Ral - ly round the flag!

CHORUS. *Melody in 2d Tenor.*

1ST. & 2D. TENOR.

Repeat pp.

Ral-ly round the flag, boys, Ral-ly round, ral-ly round, Ral-ly round the flag, boys, Ral-ly round the flag.

1ST. & 2D. BASS.

Ral-ly round the flag, boys, Ral-ly round, ral-ly round, Ral-ly round the flag, boys, Ral-ly round the flag.

Repeat pp.

ABRAHAM'S DAUGHTER.

OR

RAW RECRUITS.

1. Oh! kind folks list - en to my song, It is no i - dle sto - - ry, It's
2. Oh! should you ask me who she am, Co - lum - bia is her name, sir, She
3. They say we have no of - fi - cers, But ah! they are mis - tak - en; And

all a - bout a vol - un - teer, Who's goin' to fight for glo - ry; Now
is the child of A - bra - ham, Or Un - cle Sam, the same, sir. Now
soon you'll see the reb - els run, With all the fuss they're mak - in'; For

Copyright, 1861, by Sep. Winner.

CHORUS.

don't you think that I am right? For I am nothing short - er. And
If I fight, why aint I right? And don't you think I ought - er. The
there is one who just sprung up, He'll show the foe no quar - ter, (Mc -

I be - long to the Fire Zou, Zous, And don't you think I ought - er, We're
vol - un - teers are a pour - ing in From ev' - ry loy - al quar - ter, And
- Clell - an is the man I mean,) You know he had - n't ought - er, For

go - in' down to Wash - ing - ton To fight for A - bra - ham's daugh - ter.
I'm goin' long to Wash - ing - ton To fight for A - bra - ham's daugh - ter.
he's gone down to Wash - ing - ton To fight for A - bra - ham's daugh - ter.

4 We'll have a spree with Johnny Bull,
   Perhaps, some day or other,
And won't he have his fingers full,
   If not a deal of bother;
For Yankee boys are just the lads
   Upon the land or water;
And won't we have a " bully" fight,
   And don't you think we oughter,
If he is caught at any time,
   Insulting Abraham's daughter.

5 But let us lay all jokes aside,
   It is a sorry question;
The man who would these States divide,
   Should hang for his suggestion.
One Country and one Flag, I say,
   Whoe'er the war may slaughter;
So I'm goin' as a Fire Zou-a,
   And don't you think I oughter,
I'm going down to Washington
   To fight for Abraham's daughter.

OUR FLAG IS THERE.

This song was written by an Officer of the American Navy during the war of 1812. It being very popular, although long out of print, has been republished in compliance with the request of many Officers in the U. S. Navy.

1. Our flag is there! Our flag is there! We'll hail it with three loud huzzas! Our
2. That flag withstood the bat-tle's roar, With foemen stout, with foemen brave; Strong

flag   is there! Our   flag   is there! Be - hold   the glorious stripes and stars! Stou
hands have sought that flag   to low'r, And found   a   speedy   wat - 'ry grave! That

hearts have fought   for that bright flag, Strong hands sustained it mast head high, And
flag   is known   on ev' - ry shore, The stan - dard of   a   gal- lant band, A -

Oh !   to see how   proud it waves, Bring tears   of joy   in ev' - ry eye.
like   unstain'd in   peace or war, It   floats o'er freedom's hap - py land.

CHORUS.

Our flag is there, Our flag is there, We'll hail it with three loud huzzas, Our

Our flag is there, Our flag is there, We'll hail it with three loud huzzas, Our

melody.

flag is there, our flag is there, Be - hold the glorious stripes and stars.

flag is there, our flag is there, Be - hold the glorious stripes and stars.

WE ARE COMING FATHER ABRA'AM.

Music by L. O. EMERSON.

1. We are coming, Fa - ther Abra'am, three hun-dred thousand more, From
2. If you look a - cross the hill tops that meet the north-ern sky, Long
3. If you look all up our val-leys, Where the grow-ing harvests shine, You may
4. You have called us and we're coming, by Richmond's blood-y tide, To

Mis-sis-sip-pi's winding stream and from New England's shore; We leave our plows and
moving lines of ris - ing dust your vis-ion may des-cry; And now the wind, and
see our sturd-y far -mer boys fast forming in - to line; And chil - dren from their
lay us down for freedom's sake, our brothers bones beside; Or from foul trea-son's

workshops our   wives and children dear, With hearts to full for ut - ter-ance, with
in - stant, tears the clou-dy veil a - side, And floats a -loft our spangled flag   in
mother's knees are   pull -ing at the weeds, And learn-ing how to reap and sow,   a-
savage group,to wrench the murderous blade,And   in   the face of for-eign fces   its

but   a si - lent tear ; We   dare not look be - hind   us, but stead-fast - ly be-
glo - ry and in pride; And bayonets in the sunlight gleam, and bands brave music
gainst their country's needs; And a farewell group stands weep-ing   at eve - ry cot-tage
fragments to pa-rade ;   Six   hundred thousand loy - al men and true have gone be-

- fore.
pour,   We are   coming, Fa - ther Abra'am,   three hun-dred thousand more.
door,
- fore,

CHORUS. TENORS.

We are com - ing, we are coming, Our Un - ion to re - store, We are

BASSES.

com - ing, Fa - ther Abra'am, with three hun - dred thous and more, We are

cres.

com - ing, Fa - ther Abra'am, with three hun - dred thous - and more.

cres.

WEEPING, SAD AND LONELY.

OR

WHEN THIS CRUEL WAR IS OVER.

Words by Chas. C. Sawyer.

Music by Henry Tucker.

Moderato e cantabile.

1. Dear-est love, do you re - mem - ber, When we last did meet, How you told me that yo
2. When the summer breeze is sigh - ing Mournful - ly a - long ; Or when autumn leaves are
3. If a - mid the din of bat - tle, No-bly you should fall, Far away from those who
4. But our country called you, darl - ing, Angels cheer your way ; While our nation's sons are

loved me, Kneeling at my feet ? Oh ! how proud you stood be-fore me In your suit of
fall - ing, Sadly breathes the song. Oft in dreams I see thee ly - ing On the battle
love you, None to hear you call, Who would whisper words of comfort, Who would soothe your
fight-ing, We can on-ly pray. No - bly strike for God and lib-er-ty, Let all nations

blue,...... When you vow'd to me and coun - try Ev - er to be true.
plain, ... Lone - ly, wounded, even dy - ing, Calling, but in vain.
pain ? .... Ah . the many cruel fan - cies Ev - er in my brain.
see...... How we love the starry ban - ner, Emblem of the free.

CHORUS. TENORS.

Weeping, sad and lone - ly, Hopes and fears how vain! Yet praying,
BASSES.

When this cru - el war is o - - ver, Pray - ing that we meet a - gain!

rall

WHO WILL CARE FOR MOTHER NOW?

Arr. by C. F. THOMPSON.   Words and Music by CHAS. C. SAWYER.

During one of our late battles, among many other noble fellows that fell, was a young man who had been the only support of an aged and sick mother for years. Hearing the surgeon tell those who were near him that he *could not live*, he placed his hand across his forehead, and with a trembling voice said, while burning tears ran down his fevered cheeks, "*Who will care for mother now?*"

With expression.

1. Why am I so weak and wea - ry? See how faint my heart-ed breath, All a - round to me seems dark - ness,
2. Who will com-fort her in sor - row? Who will dry the fall - ing tear? Gen - tly smooth her wrinkled fore - head?
3. Let this knapsack be my pil - low, And my man - tle be the sky; Has - ten, comrades, to the bat - tle,

Tell me, comrades, is this death? Ah! how   well I know your an -
Who will whisper words of   cheer? E - ven now I think I see
I will like a soldier   die.   Soon with   angels I'll be march -

- swer;   To   my   fate I meek-ly   bow, ...   If   you'll
her   Kneel - ing, pray - ing for me!   how ....   Can   I
- ing,   With bright lau - rels on my   brow, ...   I   have

on - ly   tell me tru - ly,   Who   will care for mother now?
leave her in her an - guish?   Who   will care for mother now?
for my country fall - en,   Who   will care for mother now?

CHORUS. *With spirit.*

Soon with angels I'll be march - ing, With bright lau - rels on my brow, ... I have for my country fall - en, Who will care for mother now! ....

KEEP THE CAMP FIRES BURNING BRIGHT.

SONG AND CHORUS.

Words and Music by J. HENRY DWYER

Jolly.

1. Let us all be mer-ry boys, to-night, For we are here, you know, for fun;
2. Lis-ten to the speakers here to-night, Re-mem-ber, we are here for fun;
3. Cof-fee, cheese and hard-tack, that's the stuff! It gives a zest you know to fun;

Keep the glowing camp-fire burn-ing bright, For we are here to-night for fun;
Cut your speeches short, and make them light, And don't for-get we're here for fun;
Af-ter all our guests have had e-nough, Then, boys, look out for num-ber one;

Copyright, 1883, by J. Henry Dwyer

Now fill up a pipe and smoke it, Spin a fun-ny yarn and joke it,

Fill an - oth - er pipe and smoke it, Sing a mer- ry song and joke it,

Fill a part- ing pipe and smoke it, Sing a part-ing song and joke it,

SOLO OR SEMI-CHORUS.

Let us have a jol - ly, mer- ry time to-night, For we are here, you know, for fun.
We will have a jol - ly, mer- ry time to-night, For we are here, you know, for fun.
Then we'll bank the fire up, boys, and say "good-night," When we have had our fill of fun.

CHORUS.

Shout and sing, merry boys, Make a noise, jol- ly boys, We are hap-py, merry boys, And full of **fun;** So

1s & 2d. Keep the glow- ing camp-fire burn- ing bright, For we are here, to-night for fun.
Last time. Then we'll bank the fire and say "good-night," When we have had our fill of fun.

HAIL, COLUMBIA.

Written by Judge HOPKINSON, and adapted by him to the music of the "President's March."

Maestoso.

1.   Hail,   Co- lum - bia, hap- py land !   Hail, ye heroes! heaven born band! Wh‹

2.   Im-mor - tal pa- triots! rise once more· De-fend your rights; de-fend your shore: Let

3.   Sound,   sound the trump of fame !   Let   Washington's great name Ring

4.   Be-hold the Chief who now commands, Once more to serve his coun- try stands. The

fought and bled in Free-dom's cause, Who fought and bled in Free-dom's cause, And
no rude foe, with im-pious hand, Let no rude foe, with im-pious hand, In-
thro' the world with loud ap-plause, Ring thro' the world with loud ap-plause, Let
rock on which the storm will beat; The rock on which the storm will beat; But

when the storm of war was gone, En-joyed the peace your val-or won.
-vade the shrine where sa-cred lies, Of toil and blood the well-earned prize.
ev-'ry clime to free-dom dear, Lis-ten with a joy-ful ear.
arm'd in vir-tue, firm and true, His hopes are fixed on heav'n and you.

Let in-de-pendence be our boast, Ev-er mind-ful what it cost;
While offer-ing peace, sin-cere and just, In heav'n we place a man-ly trust, That
With e-qual skill, with god-like power, He gov-erns in the fear-ful hour Of
When hope was sink-ing in dis-may, When gloom obscured Co-lum-bia's day, His

Ev - er grate-ful for the prize, Let its al - tar reach the skies.
truth and jus-tice will pre-vail, And ev - 'ry scheme of bond-age fail.
hor - rid war; or guides with ease The hap-pier times of hon- est peace.
stead - y mind from chan - ges free, Re-solved on death or Lib - er - ty.

Firm, u - ni - ted, let us be, Rally-ing round our lib - er - ty;

As a band of broth- ers joined, Peace and safe - ty we shall find.

Words by HENRY S. WASHBURN.

Music by GEO. F. ROOT.

Arr. by FRANK J. SMITH.

As especially arranged for, and sung by the Lotus Glee Club, with great success, at the Concert of War Songs, in Boston, in May, 1883.

With expression.

1. We shall meet but we shall miss him, There will be one va-cant chair; We shall lin-ger to ca-ress him, While we breathe our eve-ning pray'r, When a year a-go we gathered, Joy was in his mild blue eye, But a gol-den chord is sev-ered, And our hopes in ru-in lie.............. We shall meet but we shall miss him, There will be one va-cant chair, We shall lin-ger to ca-ress him, When we breathe.......... our eve-ning pray'r.

2 At our fireside, sad and lonely,
Often will the bosom swell
At remembrance of the story
How our noble Willie fell;
How he strove to bear our banner
Through the thickest of the fight,
And uphold our country's honor,
In the strength of manhood's might

3 True, they tell us wreaths of glory
Ever more will deck his brow,
But this soothes the anguish only
Sweeping o'er our heartstrings now.
Sleep to day, O early fallen,
In thy green and narrow bed,
Dirges from the pine and cypress
Mingle with the tears we shed.

AMERICA; or, MY COUNTRY, 'TIS OF THEE.

S. F. SMITH

Maestoso.

f

dim.

1st & 2d TENOR.

1, My country, 'tis of thee, Sweet land of Lib - er - ty, Of thee I sing; Land where my
2. My na - tive country, thee, Land of the no - ble, free, Thy name, I love; I love thy
3. Let mu - sic swell the breeze, And ring from all the trees Sweet freedom's song; Let mor - tal
4. Our fathers' God, to thee, Au - thor of Lib - er - ty, To thee we sing; Long may our

1st & 2d BASS.

p

dim. p

fathers died, Land of the pilgrim's pride, From ev'-ry moun-tain side Let freedom ring.
rocks and rills, Thy woods and templed hills; My heart with rap - ture thrills Like that a - bove.
tongues awake; Let all that breathe partake; Let rocks their si - lence break, The sound pro-long.
land be bright With freedom's holy light; Protect us by thy might, Great God, our King.

f Maestoso.

1. Speed our Re-pub-lic, O Fa-ther on high! Lead us in pathways of jus-tice and right;
2. Foremost in bat-tle for Freedom to stand, We rush to arms when aroused by its call;
3. Faith-ful and hon-est to friend and to foe, Will-ing to die in hu-man-i-ty's cause,
4. Rise up, proud eagle, rise up to the clouds! Spread thy broad wings o'er this fair western world!

mf   *cres.*   *f*

Ru-lers, as well as the ruled, 'one and all, Girt Thou with virtue the ar-mor of might!
Still as of yore, when GEORGE WASHINGTON led, Thunders our war cry, we conquer or fall!
Thus we de-fy all ty-ran-ni-cal pow'r, While we contend for our Union and laws!
Fling from thy beak our dear ban-ner of old— Show that it still is for Freedom unfurled!

ff   *p*   *cresc.*   *f*

Hail, three times hail to our country and flag! Ru-lers as well as the ruled, 'one and all,'
Hail, three times hail to our country and flag! Still as of yore when GEORGE WASHINGTON led,
Hail, three times hail to our country and flag! Thus we de-fy all ty-ran-ni-cal pow'r,
Hail, three times hail to our country and flag! Fling from thy beak our dear banner of old—

Girt Thou with vir-tue the ar-mor of might. Hail, three times hail to our country and flag!
Thunders our war cry: We conquer or fall! Hail, etc.
While we contend for our Un-ion and laws. Hail, etc.
Show that it still is for Free-dom unfurled. Hail, etc.

OUR BRAVES.

Words by COL. CHAS. H. CLARKE.   M. KELLER.

1 Blest be the ground where our Braves are at rest,
  Honored each shrine where our martyrs repose,
On through the ages to come shall be bless'd,
  Those who defended our land from its foes;
Guarded our land in its war-stricken throes.
Comrades, advance in the East and the West!
  Scatter fresh garlands where martyrs repose;
  Plant the old Flag where our braves are at rest!

2 Blest be this day, bringing mem'ries so bright,
  Throughout the length and the breadth of our land,
Stout were these hearts who fought stern for the right;
  Brave were the deeds of this strong patriot band,
Valiant the heroes of our army grand!
Comrades, advance and make sacred this rite,
  Twine your fresh laurel wreaths over the land:
  Hallow this day charged with mem'ries so bright.

3 Blest thou our nation, thou God of the free,
  Vouchsafe that liberty our Fathers gave;
Guard Thou our country from sea unto sea—
  Soil which our heroes long struggled to save,
Land of our sires, and redeemed by the Brave.
Comrades, this trust keep for millions to be,
Ages to come will remember each grave;
  Cost of our nation so dear, yet so free!

MEMORIAL HYMN.

FOR MALE OR MIXED VOICES.

Words by Rev. Dr. POLLARD.   Music by A. B. WINCH.

1st & 2d TENOR, or SOPRANO & TENOR.

1. Oh, cov - er with flow - ers the val - iant dead; Let them bloom on their

1st BASS or ALTO.

3. From homes fondly cher - ish'd and friends dearly lov'd, At the call of their

2d BASS.

bo - som and wave o'er their head! Let the beau - ty and fra - grance of

coun - try they fear - less - ly mov'd; On the red fields of bat - tle they

Spring's richest bloom Fill the air that breathes o'er the dead soldier's tomb.

val - iant - ly stood, And gave for the na - tion the price of their blood.

2. In the day when re - bel - llon and trea - son were rife, And the land was con-

4. Oh, fierce was the con - flict, and cru - el the foe, And ma - ny brave

-vulsed and mad - den'd with strife, They brave - ly put on the stern

free - men his fu - ry laid low; Freedom tri - umph'd at last, and

har - ness of war, To fight for our Un - ion, for free-dom and law.

broke his fell pow'r, And rang the glad peals of sweet vic - to - ry's hour.

5.

Then cover with garlands the patriot's grave,
And perfume the rest of the faithful and brave;
Bring the beauty and fragrance of Spring's sweetest bloom,
To honor and hallow the dead hero's tomb!

6.

But no floral wreaths loving hands can entwine,
Can rival the memories, our fond hearts enshrine,
Of the noble and brave, the faithful and blest;
Honored martyrs of freedom, serene be your rest!

7.

Then glory to God who our victories gave,
And praise to the men who our nation did save;
All honor to heroes departed oe given,
Their dust rests in peace, may their souls rest in heaven!

SLEEP, COMRADES, SLEEP.

THE SOLDIERS' REQUIEM.

Words and Music by J. HENRY DWYER

1. Sleep, com - rades, sleep in calm re - pose Up -
2. To - day a grate - ful peo - ple stand A -

- on Co - lum - bia's breast;.... For thee with
- round thy hal - lowed graves,.... With loy - al

love, her bos - om glows— Rest, ye brave he - roes,
hearts and lov - ing hand, To crown "Our fal - len

rest!....... We'll deck thy bed with ro - ses
Braves".... Thy deeds up - on their souls are

ad lib.

rare— Em - blems of love and peace—......
'graved In lines of liv - ing light,.........

.... Shrined in our hearts thy mem - 'ries
.... The pa - triots of the land ye

fair Shall reign till life doth cease. ......
saved Will see that they glow bright......

To Mrs. ARTHUR CHENEY, Boston.

CONSOLATION.

HOWARD M. DOW.

1st & 2d TENOR.
p Andante.

1. Come un - to me, when shad - ows dark - ly gath - er, When the sad
2. Large are the man - sions in thy Fa - ther's dwell - ing, Glad are the

1st & 2d BASS.

Andante.

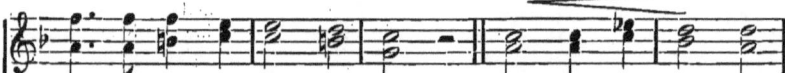

heart is wea - ry and dis - trest; Seek - ing for com - fort
homes that sor - rows nev - er dim; Sweet are the harps in

from your heavenly Fa - ther: Come un - to me, and I will give you rest.
ho - ly mu - sic swell - ing, Soft are the tones which raise the heavenly hymn

3. There, like an E - den blos - som - ing in glad - ness, Bloom the fair

flow'rs the earth too rude - ly pressed. Come un - to me, all

ye who droop in sad - ness,—Come un - to me, and I will give you rest.

WE DECK THEIR GRAVES ALIKE TO-DAY.

MEMORIAL.

Words by SAM'L. N. MITCHELL.

Music by H. P. DANKS.

1. We deck their graves a - like to - day, With blossoms fresh and fair, ... And
2. We deck their graves a - like to - day, With spring-time's fair- est flow'rs,.. And
3. We deck their graves a - like to - day, And raise our an - thems high,.... For

on the gras - sy mounds of clay, We lay the flow'rs with care; As
now and then the song - ster's lay, Makes bright the sol - emn hours; The
those who fell when far a - way, Be - neath a dis - tant sky; Our

Note. (This Quartet is preferable without accompaniment.)

o'er each sleep - ing he - ro's head, Our of - fer - ings are placed, The
vi - o - let and li - lac, sweet, Or wreath of ev - er - green, At
Coun - try call'd her gal - lant sons For ser - vice in the fray, And

brav' - ry of our hon - or'd dead, Shall nev - er be e - - rased.
eve - ry sol - dier's head and feet, Me - mo - rial Day is seen.
on the graves of fall - en ones, We strew sweet flow'rs to - - day.

COVER THEM OVER WITH BEAUTIFUL FLOWERS.

DECORATION HYMN.   E. F. STEWART.

1. Cov - er them o - ver with beautiful flow'rs, Deck them with garlands, those
2. Cov - er the hearts that have heaten so high, Beat - en with hopes that were
3. Cov - er the thousands who sleep far a - way, Sleep where their friends can - not
4. When the long years have rolled slowly a - way, E'en to the dawn of earth's

broth - ers of ours, Ly - ing so si - lent by night and by day,
doomed but to die; Hearts that have burned in the heat of the fray;
find them to - day; They, who in moun - tain and hill - side and dell,
fu - ne - ral day; When, at the an - gel's loud trum - pet and tread,

Sleeping the years of their manhood a - way. Give them the meed they have
Hearts that have yearned for the home far a - way. Once they were glow - ing with
Rest where they wea - ried, and lie where they fell. Soft - ly the grass-blades creep
Rise up the fa - ces and forms of the dead, When the great world its last

COVER THEM OVER WITH BEAUTIFUL FLOWERS.

the	past;	Give	them the	hon - ors their	fu - ture	fore
and	love,	Now	their great	souls have gone	soar - ing	a
re - pose;	Sweet - ly	a -	bove	them the	wild flow -	ret
a - waits;	When	the blue	sky	shall fling	o - pen	its

Give	them the	chap - lets they	won	in	the	strife;
Brave - ly	their	blood	to	the	na - tion	they	gave,
Zeph - yrs	of	free - dom	fly	gen - tly	o'er -	head,
And	our long	col - umns march	si - lent - ly			through,

CHORUS.

Cov - er them o - ver, yes, cov - er them over, Pa - rent and

Chorus for fourth verse.
Bless - ings for garlands shall cov - er them over, Pa - rent and

husband, broth - er and lover, Crown in your hearts those dead
husband, broth - er and lover, God will re - ward those dead

he - roes of ours, Cov - er them o - ver with beau - ti - ful flow'rs.
he - roes of ours, Cov - er them o - ver with beau - ti - ful flow'rs.

SOLDIER'S FAREWELL.

Translated from the German, by
L. C. ELSON.

JOHANNA KINKEL

1. How can I bear to leave thee, One parting kiss I give thee; And
2. Ne'er more may I behold thee, Or to this heart enfold thee; With
3. I think of thee with longing, Think thou,when tears are thronging,That

then whate'er befalls me, I go where honor calls me. Fare
spear and pennon glancing, I see the foe ad - vancing, Fare
with my last faint sighing, I'll whisper soft, while dy - ing, Fare

- well, farewell, my own true love, Farewell, farewell, my own true love.
- well, farewell, my own true love, Farewell, farewell, my own true love.
- well, farewell, my own true love, Farewell, farewell, my own true love.

I CANNOT ALWAYS TRACE THE WAY.

1st & 2d TENOR.
Religioso.

HOWARD M. DOW.

1. I can-not al-ways trace the way Where Thou Al-might-y One dost,
2. When mys-t'ry clouds my dark-ened path, I'll check my dread, my doubts re-

1st BASS.

3. Yes! God is love; a word like this Can ev-'ry gloom-y thought re-

2d BASS.

move, But I can al-ways, al-ways say, But I can al-ways, always
- prove; In this my soul sweet com-fort hath, In this my soul sweet comfort

- move, And turn all tears, all woes, to bliss, And turn all tears, all woes, to

1. move, But I can al-ways, al-ways say,
2. prove; In this my soul sweet com-fort hath,
3. move, And turn all tears, all woes, to bliss,

Can al-ways
In this my
say.... That God ... is love. 1. But I can al - ways, al -ways
hath,.... That God.... is love. 2. In this my soul, In this my
bliss,.... For God.... is love. 3. And turn all tears, And turn all
bliss,.... For God is love. And turn all
say, can al - ways say That God is love.
soul sweet com-fort hath, That God is love.
pp rit.
But I can al - ways, al - ways say that God is love.
sweet com-fort hath, sweet com-fort hath, That God is love.
All woes, to bliss, All woes, to bliss, For God is love.
tears, All woes, to bliss, For God is love.
pp rit.

SILENTLY, TENDERLY, MOURNFULLY HOME.

QUARTETTE.

Words by J. W. BARKER.　　　　　　　　　　　　　Music by N. BARKER

1st TENOR.

1. Si - lently, tender-ly, mournful-ly home, From the red bat - tle field Volunteers come,

2d TENOR.

1st BASS.

2. Si - lently, tender-ly, mournful-ly home, Where should the fallen brave Volunteers come,

2d BASS.

Not with a loud hurrah, Nor with a wild eclat, Not with the tramp of war, Come our brave sons from far.

But to his native hills, Where the bright, gushing rills Freedom's sweet music fills, And her soft dew distils!

Gently and noise-less-ly bear them a-long, Hush'd be the bat-tle hymn, music and song.

Peacefully, prayerful-ly, lay our brave friend, Close by the home that he fought to defend.

* May be sung as Alto, 8va lower.

2. Si - lently, tender-ly, mournful-ly home, Not as they marched away, Volunteers come,

4. Si - lently, fear-fully, welcome the brave, Glo - ry en - circles the patriot's grave;

Not with the sword and gun, Not with the stirring drum Come our dead heroes home, Now all his work is done.

Here let affection swell, Here let the marble tell, How the brave he - ro fell, Loving his country well.

Thoughtfully, prayerfully, bear ye the dead Pil - low it soft-ly, the Volunteer's head.

Si - lently, ten - der - ly, mournful - ly home, Welcome the Volunteers, one by one.

"OUR NATIVE LAND."

English Adaptation by M. H. CROSS.

A. BILLETER. Op. 39. No. 1.

Con spirito.

1. With hearts now touched by tend' - rest feel - ings, Oh, let us praise our na - tive land; For her we'll

2. Let ev' - - ry bless - ing now shed its fragrance, And peace and plen - ty o'er us shower; Let health and

(4pp)

sing our no-blest songs, And lav-ish gifts with o - pen

hap - pi - ness at - tend us, Till all have felt their mag - ic

hand, Oh, land with all . . . thy no - ble
power, Oh, may the bond . . . of faith and

hand, Oh land with all . . thy
power, Oh may the bond . . of

cen - - - - - - - - - - - - - - do.
for - ests, Thy plains where rug - - ged, moun - tains
kind - ness, For - ev - er hold . . us in its
no - ble for - - ests, Thy plains where rug - ged moun - tains
faith and kind - - ness, For ev - er hold us in its
cresc.
rit.
ff
stand. With God's pure sky blue mantling o'er us, Heaven bless
hand. While all thy sons shall sing re - joic - ing, Heav'n bless
a tempo. breit und ruhig.
f

thee, Our na - - tive land! With God's pure sky blue mantling

thee, Our na - - tive land! While all thy sons shall sing re -

o'er us. Heav'n bless thee, Our na - - tive land!

joic - ing. Heav'n bless thee, Our na - - tive land!

"BLEST BE THE GROUND."

W. J. D. LEAVITT.

Words by COL. CHARLES H. CLARKE. Dedicated to the G. A. R.

1. Blest be the ground where our braves are at rest. Honored each shrine. Honored each shrine where our Mar - tyrs re - pose, On through the a - ges to come shall be blest Those who de - fend - ed our land from its foes; Guard - ed our land from its trai - tor - ous foes.
2. Blest be this day bring - ing mem' - ries so bright, Thro'out the length, Thro'out the length and the breadth of our land, Stout were these hearts who fought stern for the right, Brave were the deeds of this strong pat - riot band, Val - iant the he - roes of our ar - my grand.
3. Bless thou our na - tion, thou God of the free, Vouchsafe that lib - er - ty, that lib - er - ty our Fa - thers gave; Guard thou our coun - try from sea un - to sea— Soil which our he - roes long strug - gled to save, Land of our sires and re - deemed by the brave.

Com-rades, advance in the East and the West! Com-rades, ad-
Comrades, advance and make sa - cred this rite, Com-rades, ad-
Comrades, this trust keep for mil - lions to be, Com-rades, this

vance from the East to the West! Scat - ter fresh gar - lands where
vance and make sa - cred this rite, Twine your fresh lau - rel wreaths
trust keep for mil - lions to be, A - ges to come will re -

Mar - tyrs re-pose, re-pose, Plant the old flag where our Braves are at
o - ver the land, the land, Hallowed this day charged with mem'-ries so
mem - ber each grave,each grave,Cost of our na - tion so dear, yet so

rest, at rest, Scat - ter fresh gar - lands where Mar-tyrs re - pose............
bright, so bright,Twine your fresh lau - rel wreaths o - ver the land,............
free! so free! A - ges to come will re - mem-ber each grave,............

Plant the old flag where our Braves are at rest!
Hal - low this day charged with mem' - ries so bright.
Cost of our na - tion so dear, yet so free!

BLEST BE THE GROUND.

FIRMLY STAND, MY NATIVE LAND.

NÄGELI.

With energy.

1. Firmly stand, firmly stand, my na - tive land, Firmly stand, firmly
2. Safely dwell, safely dwell, my na - tive land, Safely dwell, safely
3. Sing for joy, sing for joy, my na - tive land, Sing for joy, Sing for

stand, my na - tive land, Free in heart, and true in hand, All that's love - ly
dwell, my na - tive land, May thy sons u - ni - ted stand, Firm and true for-
joy, my na - tive land, In thee dwells a no - ble band, All thy weal to

cherish; Thus shall God remain thy friend, Then shall heav'n thy walls defend, Freedom!
ev - er; God for-bid the day should rise, When 'tis said our freedom dies! Freedom!
cherish; God with might will guard thee round, While thy steps in truth are found, Freedom!

Freedom! Freedom shall not per - ish! Firmly stand, firmly stand, Firmly
Freedom! Freedom die? Oh, nev - er! Safely dwell, safely dwell, Safely
Freedom! Freedom shall not per - ish! Sing for joy, sing for joy, Sing for

stand, firm - ly stand, my na - tive land, my na - tive land.
dwell, safe - ly dwell, my na - tive land, my na - tive land.
joy, sing for joy, my na - tive land, my na - tive land.

HOW GENTLE GOD'S COMMANDS!

From NAGELLI.

Cantabile.

1. How gen - tle God's commands! How kind his pre - cepts are!
2. His boun - ty will pro - vide, His saints se - cure - ly dwell;
3. Why should this anx - ious load Press down your wea - ry mind?

Come, cast your bur - den on the Lord, And trust his con - stant care.
That hand which bears cre - a - tion up, Shall guard his chil - dren well.
Oh, seek your heaven - ly Fa - ther's throne, And peace and com - fort find.

CAST THY BURDEN ON THE LORD.

By L. O. EMERSON.

p

Cast thy bur - den on the Lord, and he will sus - tain thee,

He will comfort thee; Cast thy bur - den on the Lord.

NEARER, MY GOD, TO THEE.

6s & 4s.

LOWELL MASON.

Religioso.

1. Near - er, my God, to thee, Near - er to thee; E'en though it
2. Though like a wan - der -er, Day - light all gone, Dark - ness be

3. There let the way ap - pear Steps un - to heaven; All that thou
4. Then with my wak-ing thoughts Bright with thy praise, Out of my

5. Or if on joy - ful wings, Cleav - ing the sky, Sun, moon and

be a cross that rais - eth me, Still all my song shall be,
o - ver me, My rest a stone; Yet in my dreams I'd be,

send - est me In mer - cy given; An - gels to beck on me
ston - y griefs, Beth - el I'll raise; So by my woes to be

stars for - got, Up - ward I fly,— Still all my song shall be,

Near - er, my God, to thee, Near - er, my God, to thee, Near - er to thee.

Near-er, my God, to thee, Near - er, my God, to thee, Near -er to thee.

Near-er, my God, to thee, Near - er, my God, to thee, Near -er to thee.